GW00633118

Garth Grose

A Verse or Two on Dartmoor

A personal view of life around Scorriton and Holne

To:- Paul & Anita. Best Wishes.

Garth Grose. March. 93.

ORCHARD
PUBLICATIONS

First published in Great Britain in 1992

Copyright © Garth Grose, 1992

ORCHARD PUBLICATIONS
2 Orchard Close
Chudleigh
Newton Abbot
Devon TQ13 0LR
Tel: (0626) 852714

British Library Cataloguing in Publication Data
CIP Catalogue Record for this book is available from the British Library
ISBN 0 9519027 1 7 (flexi)
ISBN 0 9519027 2 5 (hard back)

Designed and typeset for Orchard Publications by
Bovey Tracey TeleCentre
Courtenay House
76 Fore Street
Bovey Tracey
Newton Abbot
Devon TQ13 9AD
Tel: (0626) 835757

Printed by
Moor Print, Manaton, Devon

FOREWORD

It may be difficult for those that have not lived and worked on Dartmoor fully to understand the 'magic of the moor'. For a sailor, such as myself, the moor has much in common with the sea. It is ever changing, its moods, its shades off light and dark, and its welcome. It inspires great affection, loyalty and sometimes awe. If you understand it, and are prepared to go with its moods, it will not harm you. But if you do not understand it, and try to fight it, it can all too easily overwhelm you.

Garth Grose, the author of these poems, was born at the edge of the moor at Ashburton. His grandfather was Captain of the Henroost Mine above Hexworthy, where his father was born. After a lifetime of farming in the area, Garth and his wife Una came to Holne to run the village shop, which had once been a thriving forge.

It was a sad day for all of us in the village when they decided to take their second retirement. They were much missed, and perhaps it was that Garth and Una also missed Holne that has inspired this very personal 'Verse or Two on Dartmoor'. It presents in some twenty poems a picture that will make all those who know the area feel instantly 'at home'. For those who are strangers to Dartmoor, it provides an insight into that 'magic' that the moor instils. Its style is original and beguiling. It comes from the heart of a true 'moorman'.

It is a true privilege and pleasure for this sea man to be asked to write this foreword.

12 December 1992.   Admiral Sir James Eberle, GCB, LLD, MH.

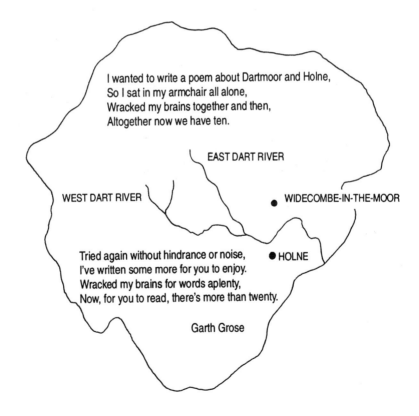

I wanted to write a poem about Dartmoor and Holne,
So I sat in my armchair all alone,
Wracked my brains together and then,
Altogether now we have ten.

EAST DART RIVER

WEST DART RIVER   ● WIDECOMBE-IN-THE-MOOR

Tried again without hindrance or noise,   ● HOLNE
I've written some more for you to enjoy.
Wracked my brains for words aplenty,
Now, for you to read, there's more than twenty.

Garth Grose

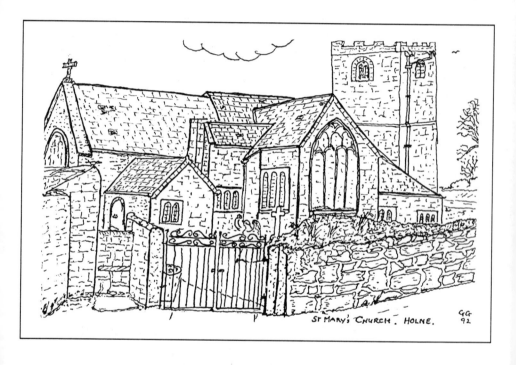

St Mary's Church. Holne.

Holne

'Holne is a delightful unspoiled village on the edge of Dartmoor, near Ashburton, and was my home for several years'.

Most times it's bleak wherever you stand,
But free is the beauty of its land.
At those great bridges one can only stare,
At mans own labour with feather and tare.

Walk for miles across peat and bog,
But keep an eye for drifting fog.
Keep an eye on horizon or road,
Or you'll not return to your own abode.

So low to land the aircraft fly,
Others journey, high in the sky.
Dartmoor high or Dartmoor low,
You can always see the snow lines show.

The skylark sings high in sunny weather,
And down below is its nest in the heather.
Try to find it if you will,
As to follow the bird will need all your skill.

Years ago there were deer and hinds,
And lots of men that worked in the mines.
High on the moor you'll find a leat
That takes you down to Holne so sweet.

Holne Church is built of granite stone,
The bells inside have their own sweet tone.
Inside the Church you'll find a lease
Of quietness and friendly peace.

And in the Inns, guitars they play,
To sing the songs of yesterday.
Johnny, Robbie, Roger and Phil
Play with everlasting skill.

So should you wish to have a treat,
Just follow down the Holne Town Leat.
Come rain or wind, whatever the weather,
You shouldn't miss this Golden Treasure.

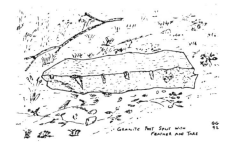

GRANITE POST SPLIT WITH
FEATHER AND TARE

The Dart Salmon

'Come the rains, to watch the salmon leap the weir near Austin's Bridge at Buckfastleigh is a quite astonishing sight'.

Far out on the moor the river Darts rise,
East and West lie under the skies.
Wending their way is quiet a feat,
Until, in unison, they meet.

Up the river the salmon run,
For fishermen they're lots of fun.
With fishing rod and home-made fly,
To catch the salmon, for hours they try.

Once the poacher there did roam,
To catch him one to carry home.
Now they poach to leave it empty,
And take them to a place of plenty.

When Dart is low and not in spate,
In pools down river they must wait.
Come the rains the salmon rise,
And leap the falls to great suprise.

To the top of the river they must go,
There to spawn for young to grow.
For ages they will toss and turn,
Some are exhausted others return.

For years your water has run the mills,
And given life to wild daffodils.
Between the trees and places to rest,
Here are the valleys you'll love the best.

Now, with heavy rain and melting snow,
Swell's you to be vicious as you flow.
In spate, O Treacherous river Dart,
Each year it's said you claim a heart.

HOLNE CHASE HOTEL.

Holne Chase

'Holne Chase Hotel can be seen from the Ashburton Road at Lent Hill, standing out clearly among the trees and commanding a beautiful setting'.

Towards the moor from Ashburton,
Holne Chase stands out like a brand new
pattern.
Above the Dart that runs so deep,
There is a place called Lovers Leap.

Down to go from Lent Hill ridge,
Where you'll encounter beautiful Holne Bridge.
People stop and look at it with awe,
For years it's harnessed Dart's vicious roar.

Here's a beauty of Dart's many vales,
The hill will test you to feel like snails.
At the top it's no suprise,
To see the view before your eyes.

Looking down see Holne curled in its nest,
The sunrise shows it at its best.
For the traveller there are things to please,
Along the road, Old Forge Cream Teas.

Beside the stream, The Village Shop,
Children play and drink their pop.
In the Church House Inn you can stay,
And forget the problems far away.

River Dart

'The River Dart flows down from High Dartmoor and gives pleasure to many, from top to bottom'

River Dart how fast you flow,
Other times so gentle and slow.
Through the woods and valleys for many a mile,
To know of your beauty, always worthwhile.

Past homestead and garden and fields of hay,
You rumble on day after day.
Raft races now, they hold every tear,
Sometimes with fear.

Canoeists, you see, relish your water,
You carry them all as part of a barter.
Day and night you go on the same,
Sometimes with company, Dart's own little train.

Up and down each day it does go,
And keeps an eye on how you do flow.
Sometimes you be low and sometimes deep,
Sometimes you seem to be fast asleep.

On past Totnes you carry your flood,
There you see Herons stood in the mud.
Now 'tis bigger boats you are expected to carry,
Pleasure and Fishing boats with Bill and Harry.

Down here it's as beautiful as ever,
You turn your corners, aren't you clever.
Soon to the sea like a lamb to the slaughter,
Tis here, *"Goodbye"* to Darts pure water.

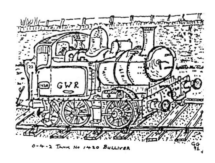

0-4-2 Tank No 1420 Bulliver

Clapper Bridge

Dartmoor on Horse Back

'I can't think of a nicer way to see the moor except on horseback, but be prepared for the weather, and preferably go with a party'.

Ride a horse if you want to see
The beauty of this high country.
Down the vale and up the steep,
Your four-legged friend will need good feet.

Your friend will need to be good and strong,
Against the elements things can go wrong.
High on the hill look afar and gaze,
You may see Princetown there in the haze.

Along here once, pack horse renown,
Carrying tin to a Stannary Town.
On Ryders Hill you couldn't ask for more,
You can almost see from shore to shore.

Ride along where the skylark sings,
And quite by chance you'll see a spring.
Your horse, like you, has got to think,
So you should stop and have a drink.

A raven once nested up on the Pupers,
Back in the days of Wheel-wrights and Coo-
pers.
Wild here is the wind and little trees bent
Not far away they held their own parliament.

Once up here a blizzard and wild,
The tragic story of a fellow called Childe.
He killed his horse to shelter in gloom,
Now there's a place called Childe's Tomb.

Down to the road, across and up the hill,
You can see in the distance the Powder Mill.
Along the vale and reaching the ridge,
Now you can see a Clapper Bridge.

Turn to the East and quietly ride,
It's still a long way to where you abide.
Granite stones, gorse and purple heather,
Dartmoor and horse gives you endless pleas-
ure.

10

The Great Ammil of 1947

'Ammil - a winter weather condition that happens only rarely on Dartmoor. It is caused by rain falling on extremely cold conditions and immediately turning to ice, covering everything it touches - a spectacular sight'.

1947 was extremely cold and hard,
All cows were kept in the yard.
Sheep with their lambs, we made little boxes,
For there to shelter, and away from the foxes.

Most of the sheep were buried in snow,
With dogs and shovels, a searching we did go.
Clever dogs, we searched, and all we did find,
The glare of the snow sent some of them blind.

The east wind was keen, froze everything around,
Our little track tractor got froze to the ground.
Layers of ice just stayed on the road,
All the way round it was very, very cold.

Below the Beacon where we did farm upon,
Came this curious Dartmoor phenomenon.
Just over night came the Great Ammil,
For acres and acres it went at will.

On a postcard a snow scene looks very nice,
But the Ammil had encased all things in ice.
Little twigs and berries encased in the freeze,
Hundreds of icicles rang a peal in the breeze.

Really the Ammil was a wonderful sight,
It glittered like thousands of stars in the night.
Nature lets the Ammil happen quite rare,
Should it happen again, you should try to be there.

Scorriton

'Scorriton, Holne's neighbouring village, has it's pub, and once, a little shop. Just like Holne, it is still unspoilt'.

Scorriton, I'm glad to say,
Still enjoys the life of yesterday.
Cows still walk up through the lane,
Till milking time and back again.

The tradesman's Arms, sometimes there's noise,
Supplied with music from the boys.
The farm next door, the geese make a row,
They had a sheep, thought it was a cow.

The dogs lie in the road and sleep,
Also here, the fox hounds meet.
Up the road is stumpy Oak,
From it's branches, crows do croak.

Each year they hold a Flower Show,
From miles around the folks do go.
Lots of stalls and things to do,
Marquee with cakes, flowers and veg's too.

Horse rides for the young ones bold,
With gentle races for the old.
Traffic lights, here not known,
Down the road a boundary stone.

If by chance you should get bored,
Stroll up the lane to Chalke Ford.
The Methodist Church there still does reign,
A big sturdy building beside the lane.

Coombe Village Hall seen it's last,
Once a school long in the past.
A bit of good advice if you're feeling low,
A good day out is Scorriton Flower show.

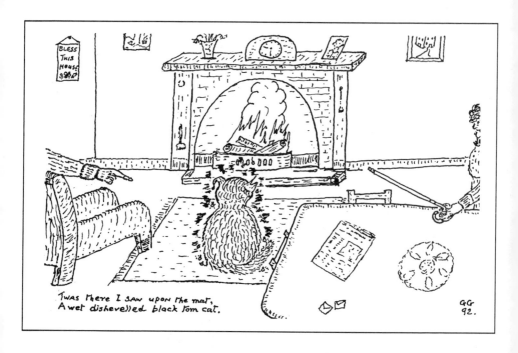

Avis Axford of Scorriton

'To Avis - a true friend to many'.

Avis Axford, you will find,
A little lady, cheerful and kind.
With groceries and papers from the shop,
'Twas always here that I did stop.

Spritely now and over eighty,
She'd say to me *'now come on matey'*
Years to work, along past the brook,
In big house service she worked as a cook.

Michael the butcher, he stopped the same,
If papers were late, I'd get the blame.
It happened sometimes, I forgot the bread,
'Wha'vee only got water in yer head?'

One day it was cold, miserable and wet.
'Come in' she cried, *'and dawn 'ee fret'*
I used to sit beside the fire,
Tell her the news or just enquire.

'Twas there I saw upon the mat,
A wet, dishevelled black tom cat.
Broken-eared and all forlon,
I bet he wishes he hadn't been born.

'How disgusting' I said, *'Is he
Out there enjoying this frivolity?'*
*'You be careful what you say about my cat,
You'm lovely precious, 'e better remember
that'.*

Laughing I went off into the rain,
I never saw the cat again.
Then one morning, wet and cold,
I saw a buzzard in the road.

I said to Avis *'I've seen your cat,
God gave him wings and now he's back'.*
'Good gracious me' Avis cried,
'One of these days I'll have your hide'!

We still go to see her, afternoon or morn,
Sit by the fire and get a warm.
Always there with a welcome smile,
People like Avis make life worthwhile.

OLD Roads Bridge before Submersion   VENFORD. RESERVOIR 1907.

GG
92

Hangman's Pit

The story of Hangman's Pit, which lies between Venford Reservoir and Combestone Tor. A triple mortar stone lies behind the old cottage at Venford'.

Early dawn, marvel at the morning skies,
Sit on Combestone Tor and see the sun rise.
Out across the land you can't resist,
To watch the valleys covered in mist.

Towards the west you see Hessary Tor,
Look around, you'll see much more.
Up through the valley it's such a treat,
Not far off the two Darts meet.

Should the rain begin to spoil your view,
Go under the rocks and take a pew.
Even the rain can bring its pleasure,
A beautiful rainbow, both ends in the heather.

Back the road there's Hangman's pit,
Once, years ago, a tragedy in it.
A man at market gambled his good horse
On an old nag. Back to face his wife, of course.

At Hangman's Pit poor man he did falter,
And hanged himself with the nag's new halter.
Along came a man, cut him down in haste,
Couldn't bear seeing a good halter waste.

Venford Reservoir lays in a valley all alone,
Water was dammed with many hand hewn stones.
Across the bridge flows a syphoned leat,
For those early days it was quite a feat.

Old road's little bridge is under the water,
Once or twice it's seen, like reservoir's daughter.
In latter years when the moor had no rain,
Lots of folks go up there just to see it again.

Go across the road and walk north east,
To Benjy Tor, you're in for a feast.
For here's a valley, one of the best on the moor,
You can sit there all day and here the Dart roar.

Buckland in the moor.

Buckland Beacon

'Take North Street from Ashburton, turn left at Great Bridge, up Hazel Hill, and the rest follows below'.

Up Hazel Hill, a gateway to the moor,
Watch out at the corners, you know the score.
Climb Welstor Hill, on your left you can see
Buckland Beacon stood there in it's own majesty.

Walk in to the Beacon getting over the stile,
On the Beacon you gasp, the view mile after mile.
The long Dart Valley between woods and clams,
Reachings way down to the far South Hams.

On big granite slabs it's here one finds,
The Ten Commandments, all carved in lines.
A man called Clements battled with the stone,
This solitary monument he carved all alone.

Down in Buckland village all covered in thatch,
Trees in the woods, home to squirrel and nuthatch.
Church clocks has numerals, I'm sure like no other,
Simply says, MY DEAR MOTHER.

Leave beautiful Buckland, on across the moor,
To go by Rippon, reach massive Haytor.
High are the rocks and lots there do climb,
To reach the summit when the weather is fine.

Long is the slope, snow brings many on a spree,
To toboggan and snowball, some try to ski.
Someone broke a leg, *'Is there a doctor or none'?*
Four doctors arrived to help out of the fun.

You may like to travel back, but not far away,
Along by the lane, the grave of poor Kitty Jay.
You'll feel your own sorrow, maybe silently pray,
For someone remembers her with flowers every day.

CHURCH HOUSE INN. HOLNE.

Holne Village

'Mr Ernie Furneaux, Captain of the bellringers and a past Chairman of the Parish Council for many years, showed me the bell tower which inspired me to write this about Holne'.

Outside Holne Church Ernie I did meet,
To go inside, see the bells for a treat.
Up the tower on little steps in a curl,
We saw the bells that peal out as they whirl.

The story of bells was cheerily told,
Inscriptions are nice, thoughtful and old.
Out on the Tower another planet,
Huge corner stones fixed with granite.

There, below, the Old Village Hall,
Once a school for Scholars all.
The coal for the fire they could not fill,
Because of an argument with Parson Gill.

To the Village Hall come the lasses,
Taking part in Keep Fit evening classes.
Every month there's the Local Council,
Try to keep things right with paper and pencil.

Altogether they do very well,
To keep the village under their spell.
In winter they scheme long after dark,
To keep the right side of Dartmoor National Park.

The Youth Club village folk do their best to please,
Young ones with energy in excess of their needs.
Cups of coffee and warm things from the cooker,
Music games and a table for snooker.

Many functions there do reside,
An archaeological dig with interesting slides.
The W.I. have their meetings and talks,
Arrange their functions and interesting walks.

Holne Grown has been a feature in latter times,
To fill your garden with flowers in lines.
Busy Fingers Ladies from all around,
Go to practise all the Arts they have found.

Court Farm, I see D.P. in consultation,
'Twas down there once an operation.
For several hours we did strive,
And kept a cow and calf alive.

Along a bit, the Old Village Forge,
Lovely cream teas for you to gorge.
Also below, the Village Shop,
Get most things there and visitors stop.

Village Farm there, with it's roof of thatch,
Cottages alongside perhaps once did match.
The Church House Inn stands there fine,
A plaque on the wall dates 1329.

Holne's Archbishop

'It was our pleasure, my wife and I, to meet Archbishop and Lady Ramsey on many occasions in the Village Shop, both before and after we rebuilt it'.

Several miles from his vocation,
Archbishop Lord Ramsey came to this location.
For thirty years or more they came,
Came to visit Holne, on a train.

In the Inn they did stay,
Take nice walks down by the way.
Rough and windy, I'll not tarry,
I think today we'll try the valley.

On the moor they liked to walk,
Here and there to stop and talk.
Stormy or rain they didn't mind,
Sometimes God's weather is unkind.

At the Village Fête, to see them 'twas nice,
In Holne Church he took Confirmation twice.
In any weather they loved to roam,
He wrote the foreword to 'A History of Holne'.

The Day's Supplies

'Some of the episodes that happened fetching the daily supplies for Holne Village shop from Ashburton'.

Travelling up with the days supplies,
Must've been cobwebs in my eyes.
Turned a corner quickly to stop,
Milk and eggs went all over the shop.

Delivering papers down in a box,
Inside a mouse gave my finger the chop.
Helped it out, it ran off in glee,
Could hear it squeaking, *'Ha ha I 'ad 'e'.*

I said to my wife, *'It should never be*
To keep such animals in captivity
Whatever it is, we'd better not linger
A vampire mouse just bit my finger'.

Driving down from Holne to Ashburton,
Chase Hill's descent never was certain.
When the four in one was a little frosty,
The quick way down could turn out costly.

In 1985, with snow on the hill,
We found out too late...boy, what a thrill!
But landed alright in a Glen at the bottom,
Never do it again, wasn't forgotten.

Early in the morning we had taken this ride,
Busy's little tail was wagging with pride.
We went on to get the bread, milk and papers
Came back through the lanes, no more of
those capers.

HOLNE 1927.

Holne Village Fête & Pantomime

'Many things go on in Holne, the most recent being the burial of a time capsule with photos and information of the present day, to be dug up in 100 years'.

The village Fête every year to see,
Lots of attractions, a nice tent for tea.
Throwing the welly, and of course, Tug of War,
One team ended up all sprawled on the floor.

Young ones dress up, Tom was a crocodile,
Nice to get a prize, they all had a smile.
In the beer tent one could host,
Or go by the fire and enjoy the Ram Roast.

Around the fire lots of folks did sit,
Bought some meat and scrounged a bit.
The Donkey Derby one year was fun,
When they set off, all ways did run.

I like to go with bowler and stick,
Enjoy the good company and get up to tricks.
Lots of draws and prizes to please, Monies
this year to Local Charities.

The Village Hall folks gave lots of time,
To produce themselves a Pantomime.
Full house, two nights, all folks did come,
To enjoy the scenes and watch all the fun.

Once a week there's a Whist Drive
Many wouldn't miss it, helps to thrive.
Also here, that I'm told,
A nice little meal for those getting old.

All these things take thought and time,
God bless those that make it their line.
Lots of old folk these days are alone,
Hope they're remembered like those up at Holne.

26

The Problems of Snow and Ice

'1947 Winter - Snow brings its problems on the farm, but it also has its humerous side too.

Up on the farm we had a blizzard,
Chilblains on me hands, nearly froze me gizzard.
Snow through the walls like a fireman's hose,
Made me shiver and get a very red nose.

Ice on the pond good and thick,
Proved it when the dog fetched a stick.
Saw a red squirrel try to climb a tree,
Ice on the bark - that fooled 'e.

A rabbit jumped out into deep snow,
Went upside down and 'e couldn't go.
Our dear old horse tried the ice like a twit,
Legs went apart and 'e did the splits.

Covered me ears and eyes when it was snowing,
Couldn't see where the heck I was going.
Ice on the meadow long and wide,
Couldn't resist to have a slide.

Fell on the ice and crashed something rotten,
Scorched me backside as I slid to the bottom.
Picked meself up and tried to hide,
Co's I'd split me trousers right down the sides.

Let out the ducks and fowls above the ice
Threw up some corn for them to entice.
They came towards me all of a wobble
Oh, my gosh! What a shamozzle!

Some went by, backside in the air,
Others with feet out streched, didn't seem to care.
The ducks sliding on belly and beak,
Trying hard to get a grip with their feet.

Slipping and sliding they all went by,
To eat some corn didn't have time to try.
On they went, several in a spin,
I wasn't quite sure which one would win.

At the speed of sound they reached the bottom,
Looked at me, in 'e rotten.
It looked to me as if they enjoyed the ride
I did, I laughed till I cried.

Return journey was equally as bad I suppose,
Have you ever tried to walk on your nose.
The laugh was back on me in a trice,
I had to carry 'em back again on the ice.

Rugglestone Inn. Widecombe.

Widecombe Fair

'Tom Pearce, Tom Pearce, lend me your grey mare, all along, down along, out along lee, for I wants to go to Widecombe fair'.

Way out o'er moor you must go,
To see lovely Widecombe far below.
Down the steep hill, go steady and gleam,
At the beautiful valley that sets the scene.

Down in the Village, a nice Village Green,
The Church looks down on it, all serene.
The Old Inn is situated over the road,
Lots of fun in there, I'm told.

Beside the lane is Rugglestone Inn,
Where men drink cider and laugh within.
A lady here does serve the ale,
I bet she could tell us a many tale.

Here by the Heath's been many a yarn,
A darn good laugh did nobody harm.
Round the table they play their Euchre
A game that baffles learner and tutor.

Once a year it's Widecombe Fair.
Folks come in droves from everywhere.
Years ago it was quieter though,
Day off for farmers and farm workers to go.

Side shows, ice cornets with cream on top,
A man took your picture, produced on the spot.
'Uncle Tom Cobley and All' were there
He rode in on his 'Old Grey Mare'.

Cart Horses and ponies with raffia and
brasses,
Paraded to find the champion in all classes.
Gymkhana was held with complicated races,
Horses and riders competed like blazes.

Pens of sheep, rams stood in their places
The judge put them all through their paces.
Some folks arrived in pony and trap,
With all the commotion the dogs use to scrap.

Tug of War brought strain to men's faces'
Big strong men with belts and braces.
When evening came, in the Village Hall,
A good end to the day, 'South Devon Hunt Ball'.

Busy

To Busy - my little Jack Russell bitch - who is now 12 years old and has accompanied me for many miles over the moor. A faithful friend'.

Up on the moor, fine rain or fog,
I love to wander with my little dog.
'Busy', she's called and loves to be free,
Searches the gorse for a rabbit you see.

When young she chased sheep. Off they did go,
She ran off after them over the snow.
Quite a long way I followed in haste,
All the way back my hand she did taste.

Now she knows to do that is wrong,
Unless she's needed to drive them along.
Once she helped to drive some big black cattle,
On my instructions she soon got 'em rattled.

'How much for yer dog'? the farmer enquired.
'Two hundred poun' until 'er gets fired'.
I'll pay 'e now yer's full whack'.
Proper job, 'cos tomorrow 'er'll be back.

A mink one day she did suprise,
Fought and killed it before my eyes.
Lucky girl, I thought, was she,
Mink generally win, better stay with me.

Chased a badger to ground one day,
Very naughty and wanted to stay.
Paid for her sins and naughty tricks,
Came out of there all covered in ticks.

Searches the moor for anything new,
Sometimes she searches, goes right out of view.
That's when I turn and sit on the track,
And watch her vigorously scenting me back.

Clever little dog and full of life,
Stayed in the shop to guard the wife.
Curled in her basket she grew a stranger,
Ears pricked up she'd growl of danger.

She's been away and travelled afar,
Miles and miles with us in the car.
But when we return she can't wait for the door
To open and let her get on with her search of the moor.

But a hawk flew down. Swallowed them for tea.

A Labour of Love

To the Misses Crowther of Warmacombe, near Buckfastleigh. A true story'.

Up in the woods, high on the ground,
Beautiful old farmhouse of granite sound.
In from the road, stone's throw from the moor,
Lives there on its own, birds encore.

This wonderful place there among the trees,
They make their own bread, honey from bees.
There at the door an archway of stone,
A little Jenny Wren had built her a home.

A place where nature really does score,
The swallows came through the front door.
To the front room, to build there would be fine,
They shut the front door. Just had to draw the line.

Enquirey one day, mouse, trap to catch,
The mice in the garden ruining the patch.
Eventually one found. Wouldn't hurt but arrest
The mice in the garden eating things they like best.

Out in the garden the trap to hide,
Soon some little mice duly caught inside.
Then far out into the woods they walked merrily,
Found a nice spot, set the naughty mice free.

Several journeys, it went on for quite a while,
The little mice were taken for a life by the stile.
Happy on their journey of mercy and love,
They hadn't seen Mother Nature lurking above.

A lovely day, a few to go free,
Mother Nature was following up there in the tree.
Off ran the little mice, how nice here to be.
But a Hawk flew down, swallowed them for tea.

'Oh dear'! they said *'What a terrible surprise
To see this carnation before our eyes'.*
Nature has worked out how to do things twice,
The mice ate the beans then the hawk ate the mice.

I don't know what happened to the trap for the mouse,
I suspect it's hanging on a nail in the house.
I hope they go on doing things like they should,
Those two lovely ladies, up there in the woods.

Princetown

'It is impossible to reach Princetown - one of the highest villages in England - without seeing the panoramic views. Unless, that is, the mist comes down to spoil your view'.

Princetown, high up in the clouds,
That cover it often in a shroud.
Little shops in the Village seek,
Log fires in the Inn do Landlords keep.

Princetown Prison, an unpleasant sight,
Dreary by day and worse by night.
Visitors stop by the wall and look,
Take a photo for their picture book.

In the Prison the convicts stay,
For their convictions they must pay.
Some work out on the prison farm,
Glad to be out and have a yarn.

Tobacco Barons they say do tout,
Which sometimes drives a convict out.
Over the wall, up goes the alarm,
But he's gone in the fog, to the nearest barn.

One chap escaped across the moor,
And nicked a bicycle from a store.
Off down the road, with no warning,
Passed a policeman, said, *'Good morning'!*

Let's leave this rather unpleasant task,
Get on the road, I'm sure you'll gasp
At the beautiful scenery, the moor is renown,
As you make your journey back to the town.

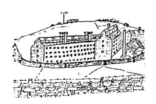

Rob The Rich

Rustlers, from time to time, take sheep and cattle off the the moor. This time it was the farmer's geese. Christmas 1948, Lr.Bowdley Farm, Ashburton'.

Up on the farm a man kept some geese,
Kept them for Christmas to have them a feast.
Most of the year they wandered around,
Eating the grass and things that they found.

All nice and fat and looking a treat,
Soon would be ready for Christmas to eat.
The gander himself a bit of a hustler,
Hadn't accounted the work of a rustler.

Someone decided that they shouldn't stay,
Crept up one night and took some away.
They left a note for the farmer to find,
The course of their action a little unkind.

He read the note and scratched his head,
And here is what the little note said.
*'We rob the rich to feed the poor,
Have left you two to breed some more'.*

Down in the Valley

'In memory of Henry French - one of the last great characters of Holne. He told me the story about the King that rode by Mitchelcombe Farm'.

Down from the moors steep on a very old road,
On horseback rode a king with armour and bold.
By a cottage he halted, saw a man past the briars,
And made it his business from him to enquire.

'Who's side are you on'? the king demanded.
The man bravely answered, as commanded.
'Not yours'! he cried from his little homestead,
He shouldn't have said it, 'cos he cut off his head.

Centuries have gone by since that trauma,
And many a tale has been told on the corner.
Big horses they drove up through the rough lane,
Worked hard in the fields, sunshine or rain.

Horses ploughed the fields, the power factor,
Before the days of the huge wheeled tractor.
Steam engines up hills and lanes took a bashing,
To reach the corn ricks, a few days thrashing.

An old man lived there, one of three brothers,
Walked with two sticks, had outlived the others.
A character and a half with his stories of foxes,
Loved his old cats and kittens in boxes.

Talked to people along the road,
Many tales he'd tell about days of old,
*'Ave 'e got a fag? I think its going to rain,
I'll 'ave two, dawn' 'spose I'll see 'e again'.*

His morning greeting was a loud *'allo'*
'You'm early an I ban ready to go'.
*'Ave 'e got what I want, I told 'e to bring
'Ang on a minute I'm gwain a check in the bin'.*

Can hear him now, *Do 'e 'ear what I say'?*
As I'd gone down the road, well on my way.
Made me laugh with the antics he supplied,
And he kept it up till the day he died.

STUMPY OAK. SCORITON.

Holne v Scorriton

Village cricket, I presume, is where the game started, and to this day it is still a joy to watch or play.

Village cricket here is provoked,
Played on the field by Stumpy Oak.
Folks from the two villages come to perform,
Been carried on since the day they were born.

One came in flannels and clean white vest,
'Din naw us 'ad to cum in fancy dress'.
Cricket pitch uneven, mole hills galore,
Made the ball wander all over the floor.

Some kept their distance from the missile,
Others sat on the ground for a while.
Bounderies worked out how far you could hit,
'Hit it that hard, better fetch it'.

Ladies were good to keep the score,
Bit one sided, add a few more.
One umpire enough, dresses up like a toff,
Any argument, red card, 'e sent 'um off.

Hands in pockets just wasn't the thing,
The ball his way didn't interest him.
Long stop a necessity in this local game,
The ball went all ways, again and again.

One ball came down at a tremendous pace,
Knocked the wickets all over the place.
Another came down and went right through,
Batsman looked back, couldn't believe it was true.

Youngs ones conversed, worked out the tactics,
Others not bothered, suffered rheumatics.
First innings all out, time for tea
Next innings, *'We'll win you'll see'.*

Farmer Webber, he did very well,
Got three out in one good spell.
Looked up the pitch, smiled in glee'
'I thought that wan would 'av 'e'.

A player decided 'e couldn't stay,
'Ad to go an pick up some hay.
'Carry on,' they said, *'No good sulking
I zoon gotta go an 'do the milking'.*

Not quite sure how the scorings stand,
Lost them all or go some in hand.
A brave little lad a high one did catch,
As it turned out, he ended the match.

Yellow Gorse

'Early morning dew on spiders' cobwebs, on a gorse bush will add another dimension to its yellow beauty, across valley and hill'.

Yellow gorse across valley and hill,
You challenge the beauty of Dart's daffodil.
Yellow gorse, prickly and strong,
All year you prove, with yellow song.

Birds use your prickly confusion,
To build their nest and avoid intrusion.
Curlew beside you, in the bog,
Release their cry in drifting fog.

Rabbits beneath you dig them a nest,
And share the place you like the best.
Little ones run beneath you and play,
Others hide under you during the day.

Sometimes you're scorched with flame,
Swaling time is here again.
Across the moor there's clouds of smoke,
But 'neath the soil new shoots you poke.

Many have tried to drive you away,
You've already decided you're going to stay.
Fern and heather help you resist,
To stay where you are you always persist.

Dartmoor, in time, sends you back again,
Strong as ever you start to reclaim.
Once more you bloom among the stone,
Dartmoor always claims back it's own.

43

Dartmoor Ponies

'The Dartmoor Pony can be seen all around the moor - their foals a delight to watch at play'.

The Dartmoor Pony, thy're bred tough,
They need to be for the weather gets rough.
Up high in the heather they have their foals,
That dance and play in little schools.

Dartmoor pony with shaggy mane,
Its forelock long, guards from the rain.
Stocky chest and good strong feet,
Clever brain, any trail they'll meet.

Commoners out on the moor keep sheep,
Gathered to dip and restrictions keep.
Gather all, not one must they leave,
To come to the attention of the Reeve.

Black cattle find grass far out in the heather,
Cross the ridge when they smell stormy weather.
Sometimes if you look when the weather is fine,
You can see them change places all in a line.

Up here alone they have their calves too,
Leave them alone and they'll not bother you.
As winter draws nigh and days are cold,
Fodder is brought to them down by the road.

Scotch sheep are timid, won't let you get near,
All run together, gallop off in fear.
They have their lambs, later together they roam,
But they don't mind because Dartmoor's home.

Other books from Orchard Publications

Along The Lemon (flexi) (reprint)	Judy Chard
A Verse or Two on Dartmoor (flexi)	Garth Grose
A Verse or Two on Dartmoor (hardback)	Garth Grose
Churches, Characters & Country Walks (flexi)	Liz Jones
Will I fly again (flexi)	Alan Brunton
Bodmin Gaol	Alan Brunton
Diary of a Country Lane	Sue Kadaw